Who Is Neil deGrasse Tyson?

by Pam Pollack and Meg Belviso

illustrated by Manuel Gutierrez

Penguin Workshop

For Arthur G. Schwartz, gerontologist helping
people live longer and healthier lives—PP

For Mason—Welcome to the universe!—MB

To all the star watchers—MG

PENGUIN WORKSHOP
An Imprint of Penguin Random House LLC, New York

The publisher does not have any control over and does not assume any responsibility
for author or third-party websites or their content.

Visit us online at www.penguinrandomhouse.com.

Library of Congress Cataloging-in-Publication Data is available upon request.

ISBN 9780399544361 (paperback)   10 9 8 7 6 5 4 3 2 1
ISBN 9780399544385 (library binding)   10 9 8 7 6 5 4 3 2 1

Contents

Who Is Neil deGrasse Tyson?

On June 30, 1973, a total eclipse covered the sun for a full seven minutes. It was the longest eclipse in more than 1,300 years. Passengers on the ocean liner SS *Canberra* watched it from off the coast of northwest Africa. But these were no ordinary cruise ship passengers. On board were two thousand scientists, engineers, and eclipse watchers. There were even two astronauts, Scott Carpenter and Neil Armstrong. The ship had been converted into a floating laboratory to do experiments during the eclipse.

Among all these grown-up scientists was one fourteen-year-old boy from the Bronx. His name was Neil deGrasse Tyson. He had won a scholarship from the Explorers Club, an association in New York City dedicated to science.

The Explorers Club allowed Neil to go on the cruise by himself. He wanted the adults to take him seriously, so he told everyone he was sixteen.

On board the ship, Neil listened to talks

given by scientists. He watched and took part in experiments. And he looked at the stars through the Criterion Dynascope telescope that he brought with him. The cruise lasted for fifteen days.

One night on the journey home, there was a trivia contest for the scientists aboard. They were grouped into teams of four or five. They had to answer all kinds of questions about the universe. One by one the teams dropped out, stumped by questions like "Which day of the year can never have a solar eclipse?" and "What are the correct names of objects or aliens from Mars, Venus, and Jupiter?"

Finally, there were only two teams left. Neil was on one of them. The pressure was on. Neil didn't want to let his team down. The man leading the trivia contest read the last question into a microphone. Whichever team knew the correct answer would win. The final question was: "What feature of the planet Saturn, other than its beautiful ring system, strongly distinguishes it from all other planets in the solar system?"

Neil broke into a big smile. He loved everything about the universe and his favorite planet of all was Saturn. There was little he didn't know about it. The other contestants, some of them respected professional scientists, looked at one another. None of them knew the answer.

Neil stood up and raised his hand. All heads turned to the teenager with the Afro. "Saturn,"

he said clearly, "is the only planet with an average density less than water." In other words, if you dropped Saturn into a giant bathtub, it would float.

"Correct!" said the host. The room burst into applause. Neil had won a bottle of champagne for his team and he wasn't even old enough to drink it.

CHAPTER 1
Skyview

Neil deGrasse Tyson was born in Riverdale, a neighborhood in the Bronx borough of New York City on October 5, 1958. His father, Cyril, was a college professor and a sociologist. That meant he studied how human beings lived together. When Neil was born, his Puerto Rican mother, Sunchita, was a stay-at-home mom raising Neil and his older brother, Stephen.

When Neil was four, his parents had another baby, his little sister, Lynn. They lived in an apartment complex called Skyview on a high hill, close to the Hudson River.

When Neil was nine, his parents took him and his brother and sister to the Hayden Planetarium. The Hayden Planetarium is part of the American Museum of Natural History. The museum is dedicated to studying the natural

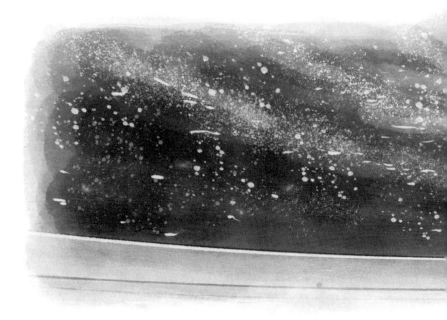

world. It displays fossils of dinosaurs, models of animals from all over the world, and minerals from deep in the earth. A planetarium is dedicated to the study of outer space: stars, planets, and distant galaxies. Neil sat under a dome that showed a projected re-creation of the universe. Neil looked up at the thousands of tiny stars and thought, *This isn't real.*

Hayden Planetarium

The Hayden Planetarium opened in 1935 in New York City, thanks to a donation from a man named Charles Hayden. It's goal was to give the public "a more lively and sincere appreciation of the magnitude of the universe . . . and for the wonderful things which are daily occurring" there. Visitors could sit in a domed theater that looked like space itself. The planetarium has been featured in many movies and TV shows set in New York, including *Night at the Museum: Secret of the Tomb* and *Men in Black II*. In 1997, it closed and was demolished. A new and improved Hayden Planetarium opened in 2000, along with the Rose Center for Earth and Space. The planetarium looks like a giant orb that seems to float. It houses two theaters: the Star Theater and the Big Bang Theater, which demonstrates the birth of the universe.

The Bronx is one of the five boroughs of New York City. Residents of New York don't see stars when they look up at the night sky because the city is so bright and filled with electric light. When all that light is reflected by gas and particles in the atmosphere, the stars fade away. This unique situation is called sky glow. Neil had lived his whole life surrounded by sky glow, so he barely saw any stars. He thought the stars in the planetarium were a fantasy, like the TV show *Star Trek*.

After his trip to the planetarium, Neil's family visited Pennsylvania. One night, standing on a mountain, Neil looked up and saw a night sky that looked just like what he had seen at the Hayden Planetarium. At that moment, he knew he wanted to learn more about the universe.

Neil's teachers wished he would pay more attention to the things he was studying in school. "Neil should cultivate a more serious attitude toward his schoolwork," one of them wrote on his report card. Another teacher thought he spent too much time talking to other kids and not enough studying. At a parent-teacher conference, Neil's mom was told, "Your son laughs too loud." But Neil loved having fun with his friends, so he didn't stop laughing.

His best friend was Phillip Branford, who lived in a nearby building. He and Phillip were often at each other's apartments. In July 1969, Phillip took Neil on a trip to visit his relatives in Virginia. Neil was ten years old. Together, the two boys watched on TV as the first humans walked on the surface of the moon.

The First Moon Landing

On July 20, 1969, the Apollo 11 spacecraft landed on the moon. It was the first time in history that humans had reached the moon. The astronauts aboard were Buzz Aldrin, Neil Armstrong, and Michael Collins. Buzz and Neil landed on the moon together in the Apollo Lunar Lander called *Eagle*.

Neil Armstrong let the world know "The *Eagle* has landed."

Then the world watched a broadcast straight from the spacecraft as Buzz and Neil stepped out onto the moon's surface. They planted an American flag in the soil of the moon. Neil said, "That's one small step for a man, one giant leap for mankind."

Sometimes, Neil and Phillip went up to the roof of one of their buildings. One night, Phillip brought a pair of binoculars. Neil had only ever used binoculars to watch sports, but on this night, Phillip suggested he look up at the sky.

When Neil pointed the binoculars at the crescent moon, he couldn't believe his eyes. It was not just bigger, he thought, but better. He could see the shadows of craters and valleys and hills on the moon's surface.

Many scientists had already seen what Neil was seeing on the moon. But for Neil, it was as if he had just discovered a new world. A world he wanted to know everything about. He wanted to study it in detail. In that moment, Neil knew what he wanted to do when he grew up. He wanted to study the universe. He didn't yet know what that was called, but he soon found out: Neil wanted to become an astrophysicist.

CHAPTER 2
A New Explorer

An astrophysicist studies what stars and planets are made of and how they came to be. They try to learn why and how they move through space. An astrophysicist needs a good telescope to magnify the image of objects in space at which to get a closer look. To earn the money for his telescope, Neil offered to walk the dogs for his neighbors in the building. He quickly earned about two-thirds of the money to pay for the telescope. His parents paid the rest. Neil's telescope was called a Criterion Dynascope. He said it looked like "a cross between an artillery cannon and a grenade launcher."

Neil started taking his telescope up to the roof of the building, often making his little sister help him carry it. A neighbor on the top floor let Neil plug the long extension cord in at his apartment. Neil was amazed at how different the night sky

looked through it. Later, he would describe looking through his telescope as astonishing: "Saturn has rings! Oh my gosh, the moon has craters! Things that you've heard about and read about—but to experience them yourself becomes a singular moment in your life."

Sometimes, people in other buildings noticed Neil on the roof. More than once they called the police because they thought he was a burglar! When the officers arrived, Neil let them have a look through his telescope.

School became a lot more interesting for Neil, and his grades improved. One teacher noticed that all of Neil's book reports were about space. One day, she gave him an advertisement she had clipped out of the paper. It said that the Hayden Planetarium was offering classes about astronomy. She suggested Neil take one called "Advanced Topics in Astronomy for Young People." The class was for kids a few years older than fourteen-year-old Neil, but she thought he could handle it.

The Hayden Planetarium was the place where Neil had first seen the night sky full of stars. The classes he took there showed him that there was a much bigger universe even beyond the stars. He attended classes there regularly on the weekends or after school and applied what he learned to his schoolwork. In shop class in seventh grade, all the students had to a build a lamp. They were given several designs to choose from, but Neil designed his own lamp based on his favorite planet, Saturn. The switch to turn the lamp on and off was a tilt of Saturn's ring.

Saturn

Saturn is the sixth planet from the sun and the second largest planet in the solar system, behind Jupiter. If you put nine Earths side by side, it would *almost* be as wide as Saturn, not counting the seven rings that surround it. Saturn's rings are made up of chunks of ice and rock. The planet itself is a massive ball of gas, mostly hydrogen and helium. It orbits the sun from about 886 million miles away.

Saturn has fifty-three known moons with twenty-nine more waiting for verification. It's named for the Roman god Saturn, whose name also inspired the word *Saturday*.

At fourteen, Neil was always the youngest person in his planetarium classes. Many of the other students were adults, like Vernon Gray. Vernon was the director of education at the Explorers Club in Manhattan—a society for scientists, explorers, and people who loved science. During a break in the class one day, Neil began asking the teacher questions about black holes, regions of space where the gravity is so strong, everything is sucked into it. Vernon heard Neil's questions, gave him his phone number at the Explorers Club, and suggested Neil call him.

Neil put Vernon Gray's card in his pocket. He didn't know what to do with it. But when he got home and showed the card to his mother, she knew this was a great opportunity. Obviously, Vernon Gray thought Neil should be in the club, and she called him right away.

Vernon told Neil about the scholarships the club offered. He thought Neil should apply for one of the educational experiences that the club paid for. Neil was fourteen, and he decided to apply. He was given a scholarship to join his first scientific expedition. Neil was going to Africa!

The Explorers Club

The Explorers Club was founded in 1904 in New York City, bringing together explorers of all kinds. Its members have gone to the North and South Poles, the summit of Mount Everest, the bottom of the ocean, and the surface of the moon. Some of its most famous members are Teddy Roosevelt, Robert Peary, and Neil Armstrong.

Today, the club has about 3,500 members all over the world. They include people in many fields, from oceanography to diving to paleontology. Because it is dedicated to creating new generations of scientists and explorers, the Explorers Club offers scholarships to high-school and college students.

CHAPTER 3
On the SS *Canberra*

The SS *Canberra* sailed from New York City on June 22, 1973, and traveled to the coast of Mauritania in northwest Africa. On June 30, the passengers watched from the deck as the shadow of the moon covered the sun for five minutes and forty-four seconds.

Those were the most exciting minutes of the trip, but the other fourteen days were filled with lectures, experiments, and stargazing. It was like a mini-university, and Neil loved every minute. He was the youngest person aboard—and he was learning a lot.

There were two thousand other passengers on the ship: scientists, engineers, and other eclipse fans, including two astronauts, Neil Armstrong and Scott Carpenter. Also aboard was a famous science fiction writer, Isaac Asimov.

Neil Armstrong and Scott Carpenter

Isaac Asimov (1920–1992)

 Isaac Asimov was born in a small town called Petrovichi in Russia. His family came to the United States when he was three years old. He grew up working in his parents' candy store in Brooklyn. He loved to read the science fiction comic books that were sold there. As an adult, he taught at Boston University. But he was most famous for his science fiction stories. He wrote or edited more than five hundred books—science fiction and popular science titles.

He's most known for his Foundation series, a total of seven books published between 1942 and 1993. Asimov is also known for creating the three rules of robotics, the laws by which robots should operate.

Neil had such a good time on the Explorers Club trip that he went on another trip later that summer. This time he was lucky enough to go to Camp Uraniborg in the Mojave Desert in California. The students stayed up each night until the early morning, looking through their telescopes at the clear desert sky.

Neil in the Mojave Desert

On the way home, they stopped at a meteor crater outside Flagstaff, Arizona, not far from the Grand Canyon. It was a hollow in the ground nearly a mile across and about 560 feet deep. In the 1960s, scientists had figured out that the crater was created more than fifty thousand years

Arizona's Meteor Crater

earlier when a massive meteor—a giant space rock—collided with Earth. The crater became one of Neil's favorite places in the world. "You can bury a sixty-story building in the middle of that crater," he said later. "It's a reminder of the awesome power of the universe."

These trips made Neil more enthusiastic than ever about science. A family friend who taught at an adult education school was so impressed hearing him speak that she recommended him to a colleague who invited Neil to give a lecture at a science workshop. Neil, whose teachers once said he talked too much in class, found that he loved teaching.

Comet Kohoutek was in the news at this time. A comet is an icy space object that releases gases as it passes the sun. The gases make the comet look like it has a tail. Scientists knew that the comet they named Kohoutek would soon be visible in the sky in 1973 for the first time in 150,000 years. People were excited about it, so Neil decided to teach his class about comets.

Although he was only fifteen and he'd never taught a class before, Neil wasn't the least bit nervous. For him, nothing could be nicer than talking about the universe. Three days after the lecture, Neil received a paycheck of fifty dollars and an invitation to give two more lectures.

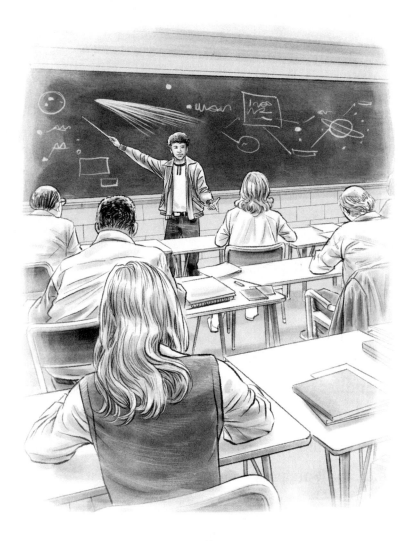

More scholarships and trips followed, including one with Educational Expeditions International to Kilmartin, Scotland. There, Neil studied prehistoric megaliths—large stones that ancient peoples used to build structures

or monuments. Scientists had realized that the prehistoric builders had constructed these huge monuments to line up with star appearances and formations. Neil analyzed and surveyed how.

In high school, Neil attended the Bronx High School of Science. It was a public school, but to get in, students had to take a very difficult exam. At Bronx Science, Neil loved to dance. And he picked up a new hobby: wrestling. He was strong and athletic, but he also had a secret advantage. He understood physics. Physics is the branch of science that focuses on energy. It includes the study of things like speed, movement, and gravity. This came in very handy in wrestling, where Neil could calculate just how to balance himself and push his opponent to flip him over.

Neil became the editor in chief of the *Physical Science Journal* at school. It was a publication written entirely by students, with articles, puzzles, and graphics about science. Students at the school also produced journals on other subjects, including a literary magazine and a math bulletin.

Neil's version of the *Physical Science Journal* was sixty-four pages, the longest journal the students had ever produced.

Neil was very busy during his high-school years. But it was getting close to the time for him to start thinking about choosing a college.

Neil D. Tyson, 546-1789, 5700 Arlington Ave., Bronx, N.Y., 10471
Captain of the Wrestling Team, Editor — Physical Science Journal, Astronomy Club, Physics Prep. Squad.

CHAPTER 4
The Space Between the Pumpkins

When Neil began applying to colleges, he created a special system. He had a subscription to the magazine *Scientific American*. The magazine always included an "About the Authors" section that gave a lot of personal information about the people who wrote the articles, always listing where they had gone to school. Neil counted up all the articles about physics and astronomy he read and noted what colleges and universities their authors had attended. He then applied to the schools that appeared most often.

After refining his list, Neil applied to five schools. His top three choices were Harvard University, Cornell University, and the Massachusetts Institute of Technology, or MIT. Cornell was where one of Neil's personal heroes taught, a professor named Carl Sagan.

Cornell University

Carl Sagan (1934–1996)

Carl Sagan was born in Brooklyn, New York. His father was a garment worker from Ukraine. His mother was from New York. He grew up to be a professor at Cornell University and a scientist. But he was best known as a science communicator—someone who could explain difficult concepts to people who didn't study science. He wrote books that educated people about scientific ideas.

His TV series *Cosmos* ran in 1980 and is still popular today.

Carl was very interested in the possibility of life on other planets. He created the first messages that were sent into space to be understood by alien life forms. The first is the Pioneer Plaque, placed on board the Pioneer spacecraft traveling through the universe. The other was the Voyager Golden Records, recordings intended to show the diversity of life on Earth. Carl wrote a novel about messages from Earth being heard in space called *Contact*, which was made into a movie in 1997.

Neil didn't know it, but the admission office at Cornell was so impressed by his enthusiasm about the universe that they sent his application letter to Carl Sagan personally. Neil was shocked when he got a personal letter from Carl inviting him for a private visit in Ithaca, New York, where Cornell is located. Neil couldn't believe it. Carl Sagan, the scientist he had seen on television, and who had written some of his favorite books, wanted to meet him!

Neil met Carl Sagan in December 1975. Even though he was a famous scientist, Carl seemed to be truly interested in Neil and what he could accomplish in the future. When he left, Carl even gave Neil his home phone number in case the bus wasn't able to drive through the heavy snow in upstate New York. For the rest of his life, whenever Neil talked with a student, he tried to be as kind and interested as Carl Sagan had been to him.

As much as Neil loved his trip to Cornell, he decided to go to Harvard, the school that had the most authors represented in *Scientific American*. He was excited to study science, but there were plenty of other things to do at Harvard as well. Neil joined the rowing, wrestling, and dance teams.

At Harvard, Neil noticed that many students he met assumed that he was attending the school on a sports scholarship. They were surprised to learn that he majored in physics, the study of nature, matter, and energy. He thought this was because he was Black and there just weren't many famous Black scientists. That made Neil determined to change people's awareness about people of color in scientific fields.

One day, another Black student told Neil he should consider switching his major. He thought, as a Black student at Harvard, Neil should want to work in something like government where he would be directly improving society, especially to make it more equal. But Neil knew how important science could be. He hoped one day to help other people understand that.

And Neil did try to help people. He joined a program where once a week he went to a prison in Walpole, Massachusetts, to tutor the prisoners there. He helped them pass the math sections of their GEDs, a test to prove high-school knowledge and gain a diploma. He found that some prisoners just wanted someone to talk to. Neil was surprised at how much he sometimes had in common with them. One inmate even had the same favorite album Neil did, Marvin Gaye's *What's Going On.*

During his years at Harvard, Neil was required to take an art class. For weeks, the class drew nothing but pumpkins. Neil got pretty good at it. Then the teacher announced, "Draw the space *between* the pumpkins." At first Neil was confused. Then he was excited.

He had a whole new way of looking at the universe! He thought of all the shapes and forms and spaces in between. He thought every scientist should take art classes.

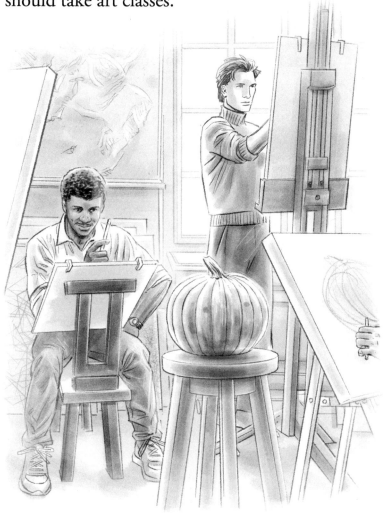

In the spring of 1980, Neil's four years at Harvard were coming to an end. He was featured, along with the 130 other Black students in his graduating class of 1,600, in a *New York Times* article. The newspaper predicted great things from them. Neil planned to prove them right.

CHAPTER 5
Physics in Action

Neil had graduated from Harvard, but he was not finished with school. He went on to study astronomy at the University of Texas in Austin. Astronomy was an important part of astrophysics. He also kept up with his other hobbies, joining the ballroom dance team and helping them win a gold medal in a national tournament.

In 1980, one of Neil's heroes, Carl Sagan, got his own TV show. For thirteen episodes, *Cosmos* was like nothing that had been seen on TV before. It taught regular people about exciting scientific ideas, such as where life began on Earth and how stars are formed and how they die. The series used special effects to make Sagan appear to be walking on distant planets. But what was really amazing about *Cosmos* was how many people loved it then and still do today.

Even thirty years later, it remained one of the most widely watched Public Broadcasting Service (PBS) series in the world. For Neil, it was proof that everyday people could be excited by science. He was glad there were people like Carl Sagan to encourage them.

As a graduate student, Neil had to take classes and also work as a teacher's assistant. He helped grade papers and sometimes taught classes for other professors. He looked up to the professors for whom he worked so that he could learn how to be a better teacher himself. A professor named Frank N. Bash became his role model. Professor Bash taught him that it wasn't enough for a teacher to just tell students what they needed to know.

Professor Frank N. Bash

He had to make sure the student understood what they were learning. He taught his students how to think deeply about the subject. Neil wanted to be a teacher like Professor Bash, trying out what he learned from him when he tutored high-school students in math for extra money. More and more, Neil was discovering how much he loved sharing his love of science with others.

While at graduate school, Neil found a new place to share his enthusiasm. He started writing a column in *StarDate*, a magazine published by the University of Texas observatory. In his column, Neil answered questions about the universe.

The name *StarDate* was chosen to echo the opening words of the TV show *Star Trek*.

In one of Neil's physics classes, he met another graduate student, Alice Young. Alice was studying mathematical physics. That meant she used math to represent things in the physical world, such as how strongly objects are drawn to each other by the force of gravity.

Star Trek

Star Trek first premiered on American TV on September 8, 1966. It followed the journey of the starship *Enterprise* and its crew, led by Captain James T. Kirk, chief science officer Mr. Spock, and chief medical officer Dr. Leonard McCoy. The action took place in the future—in the years of the 2260s.

The original series began with the voice of Captain Kirk talking about "Space: The Final Frontier" and vowing to "boldly go where no man has gone before." Each episode included the captain making an entry in his captain's log tagged by its "star date," a fictional time system that had been invented for the show.

The series only ran until 1969, but its fan base was so enthusiastic that they kept the show alive, writing their own stories and planning meetings. *Star Trek* inspired a later series of movies and more TV shows, including *Star Trek: The Next Generation* (1987–1994), *Star Trek: Deep Space Nine* (1993–1999), and *Star Trek: Discovery* (2017–present).

Neil noticed Alice right away. She sat in the front row. Eventually Neil introduced himself and asked her out. While they were dating, they both traveled to a conference on the Amalfi Coast of Italy. After the conference was over, Neil and Alice traveled around Italy together. One day, their tour bus got stuck outside a small village. Someone had parked a car too far out into the narrow road. The bus couldn't pass by. The driver honked and honked but the car's owner didn't come. More cars lined up behind the bus.

Neil took this opportunity to demonstrate physics in action. He got out of the bus and went to the car. Because of his studies, he knew just how to slide the car by himself. He moved it over a few feet to give everyone room to pass, then got back on the bus. When he was finished, everyone on the bus and those watching from the village burst into applause.

As they drove away, Neil thought that he might one day become a legend in this village: the tall Black superhero who moved a car by himself. But Neil knew he didn't have superstrength. He just understood physics.

CHAPTER 6
New Horizons

Neil and Alice got married in 1988, right after Neil had spent a year teaching astronomy at the University of Maryland. Alice had continued to study at the University of Texas and earned a PhD in mathematical physics. A PhD is a degree that stands for Doctor of Philosophy. To earn a PhD, a student must write a paper, called a thesis, which contributes an important and original idea about their subject.

After teaching at the University of Maryland, Neil decided to study for a PhD in Astrophysics at Columbia University in New York City.

Neil's thesis—his biggest project—was about galactic bulge, the fact that the stars in the middle of a galaxy are closer together than those at the far ends.

Astrophysics

Astrophysics is the study of what the universe is made of, and the laws of physics that describe—and even predict—how and why the stars and planets move the way they do.

An astrophysicist might study the possibility of time travel, multiple universes, or wormholes (shortcuts between two places separated by space and time). They also study complex material in the universe like dark matter, regions like black holes, and ideas like how universes evolve over time.

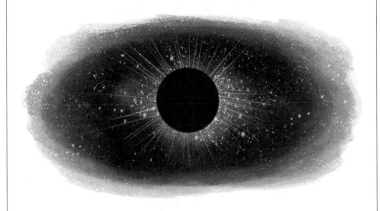

In 1989, Neil collected the letters he'd written in *StarDate* magazine and published them all together in a book called *Merlin's Tour of the Universe*. Although Neil didn't know it at the time, his book caught the attention of some people who worked at the Hayden Planetarium. They were looking for a young scientist to run the planetarium. They thought Neil might be a good choice.

Neil had been busy promoting his book and doing interviews on television. He began thinking about all the scientists he had seen on TV when he was a young boy. Not one of them had been Black. He hoped that there were Black children seeing him on TV now. He wanted to be able to inspire them to consider studying science, too.

He hoped to one day have a job that could show how exciting science was for all people.

In May 1991, Neil got his PhD from Columbia.

Neil graduates from Columbia University

He was offered a position at Princeton University in New Jersey. For three years, Neil gave lectures to students who were studying astrophysics there. Sometimes, he went to the gym to wrestle with the Princeton team, just for fun.

In his last year at Princeton, Neil was invited by the Public Broadcasting Service to appear in an episode of a TV show called *Breakthrough: The Changing Face of Science in America* about scientists outside of their labs and classrooms.

The show followed Neil on a trip to the Cerro Tololo Inter-American Observatory in the Andes Mountains of South America. They also filmed him wrestling in the gym.

Cerro Tololo Inter-American Observatory

Shortly after the program aired on television, Neil got a call from the Hayden Planetarium, the place where he'd seen his first stars as a boy. The planetarium asked him to join their staff. They hoped Neil would bring new ideas for exhibits and help them redesign the planetarium in a way that would be exciting for young visitors. If there was one person who knew about getting people—especially young people—interested in science, it was Neil.

CHAPTER 7
Goodbye, Pluto

Neil got right to work thinking up new exhibits for the Hayden Planetarium. When he first started in July 1994, he was a staff scientist working part-time because he was still teaching at Princeton. Just two years later, he was named director of the whole planetarium. At thirty-eight,

he was the youngest person to ever hold that position. That same year, Neil and Alice had a daughter, Miranda. She was named after the smallest of the planet Uranus's five major moons.

The planetarium closed down in 1997 for major renovations. The whole building was being torn down and then rebuilt. As director, Neil oversaw all the renovations. The new building would be a six-story-high glass cube enclosing an eighty-seven-foot illuminated sphere that looked like it was floating. One of the two men who designed it called it a "cosmic cathedral." Kids who came to look at the stars

the way Neil did as a boy would now sit in the top half of this floating globe and get to see a three-dimensional picture of the universe based on images from a supercomputer. In the bottom half of the sphere was the Big Bang Theater. The audience there would sit in an eight-foot-deep bowl with a thirty-six-foot-wide screen and watch a four-minute movie about the birth of the universe.

The Big Bang

Georges Lemaître

The big bang theory was developed by an astronomer named Georges Lemaître in 1927. Today, it is the most widely-accepted explanation of how the universe began.

Lemaître believed the entire universe had started as just a single point made up of tiny particles, light, and energy. The particles grouped together and formed atoms. The atoms formed molecules that eventually grew into the universe by constantly expanding. Scientists believe the universe is 13.8 billion years old, and that it's still expanding.

Neil was busy overseeing all the work on the new planetarium, including a timeline of the history of the entire universe that visitors could walk along. But he still found time to write an essay in *Natural History Magazine* in February 1999. The essay was called "Pluto's Honor." It was about the ninth planet in our solar system, the one farthest from the sun. Neil argued that Pluto wasn't really a planet. It was more like a comet, he thought. It was too small—even Earth's moon was bigger. More than half of Pluto was made of ice. If it ever drifted as close to the sun as Earth is, Pluto would

Pluto

grow a hundred-million-mile cometlike tail as the ice melted. If other scientists believed Neil's theory, Pluto would be downgraded from being the tiniest planet in our solar system to the largest known icy object there.

The new planetarium opened to the public on February 19, 2000. It was now part of a big educational center called the Frederick Phineas and Sandra Priest Rose Center for Earth and Space (sometimes simply called the Rose Center).

Visitors to the new planetarium's display of planets would still find Pluto—but not in the planets display. Neil had grouped it with the other icy objects floating beyond Neptune.

In 2000, the International Astronomical Union named an asteroid they'd discovered in 1994 after Neil in recognition of his important work. It's called 13123 Tyson. Having an asteroid named after him was exciting, but Neil had something even better in his life: a son, named Travis! He was born in 2001. At work and at home, Neil's life was expanding.

CHAPTER 8
A Wider Audience

Neil and his family lived on the south end of Manhattan in New York City. Their apartment was four blocks away from the World Trade Center, also known as the Twin Towers because of its two nearly-identical skyscrapers. On the morning of September 11, 2001,

World Trade Center

a group of terrorists took over several airplanes. They wanted to use them to attack important buildings in the United States, including the Twin Towers. They flew one plane into each tower. The buildings collapsed.

For the next twelve days, Neil's family moved in with his parents, who now lived just outside of New York City. They couldn't stay in their apartment because of all the dust and debris from the wrecked buildings. Even after they returned home, Neil found it difficult to walk along the street with five-year-old Miranda and baby Travis. When he saw the spot where the Twin Towers used to be, he remembered the terrible day when they had to run from their home. Neil had spent his life helping people see the wonder of the world and universe around him. He couldn't understand why people would want to destroy it.

A few weeks after the attack, Neil went to a meeting at the White House. He spoke with scientists and congressmen about the future of air and space travel. In 2004, Neil was awarded NASA's highest honor, its Distinguished Public Service Medal.

Neil was becoming more and more well-known to the public. PBS thought he would make a great host of a new four-part TV show they wanted to produce, called *Origins*. It asked the question of how the universe and life on Earth itself might have started. The show had a website especially for middle-school and

high-school science students. Neil wrote an *Origins* book with Donald Goldsmith, an astronomy writer who had worked on the show *Cosmos*, starring Carl Sagan.

NASA

The National Aeronautics and Space Administration (NASA) was founded in 1958 by President Dwight D. Eisenhower. It is an agency of the US government that oversees the civilian space program. Their missions have included crewed flights to the moon and the exploration of Mars and the universe beyond on uncrewed robotic missions. In addition to its space missions, NASA also studies Earth itself as seen from space. It's also a member of the International Space Station program, working closely with agencies representing Russia, Japan, Europe, and Canada to create research laboratories that orbit our planet.

It turned out Neil was a great host. So the next year, PBS asked him to host a show called *NOVA scienceNOW*. That show covered all sorts of scientific subjects from how the brain works to the life of dinosaurs to the question of whether a person could live forever.

In early 2005, Neil heard about a new discovery in space, one that had special meaning for him. Scientists at the California Institute of Technology discovered a giant object floating beyond Neptune. It was much bigger than Pluto. To the public, this object seemed like proof of a tenth planet.

But to scientists, it seemed like proof that Pluto wasn't actually a planet, just as Neil had said years earlier. The discussion continued until August 2006 when the International Astronomical Union, an international association of astronomers who were considered the authority on defining objects in space, decided to make

clear what counted as a planet. According to the new definition, a planet must: (1) orbit around a sun, (2) be massive enough to be pulled into a round shape by its own gravity, and (3) have cleared the area around its orbit. That is, there can't be any other big objects around it, unless those objects are orbiting it.

International Astronomical Union 2006 General Assembly

Since Pluto did not fit the third definition, it was officially declared a dwarf planet. Neil was right after all. In January 2009, Neil published Pluto's story in a book called *The Pluto Files: The Rise and Fall of America's Favorite Planet.*

CHAPTER 9
A Visit from Superman

On June 1, 2009, Neil began hosting a new podcast called *StarTalk Radio*. A podcast is a recording that people can listen to on their phones or computers. Fans can subscribe to the show so that new episodes are automatically sent to them.

Climate Change

The word *climate* describes weather conditions over the long term in a certain region. It is different from *weather*, which is local and temporary.

For the last few decades, the earth's climate has been changing faster than at any other time scientists know about from their studies. It's getting warmer—everywhere. The rising temperatures cause sea levels to rise, animal extinctions, extremes of

weather like flooding and forest fires, heat waves and droughts.

What is causing this change? Scientists have discovered that it's humans. When we started burning fossil fuels (coal, oil, and natural gas) we released harmful gases into the atmosphere that act like a blanket, trapping heat close to Earth. The term "climate change" generally refers to the warming of Earth's atmosphere.

StarTalk was a show about astronomy and physics, but it was also funny. Neil talked to scientists, politicians, and celebrities about all sorts of subjects, including climate change, telescopes, and movie special effects. Neil hoped the show would bridge the gap between science, pop culture, and comedy. He wanted to show people that science was part of life and fun to learn about. Neil liked to say the show was about "everything under the sun; or rather under the universe!"

That same year, in 2009, Neil joined Twitter— a social media platform where users post short comments. When Neil joined, a Tweet could be no longer than 140 characters. That meant no more than 140 letters, spaces, or punctuation marks. Neil has over fourteen million followers on Twitter.

Follow

Neil deGrasse Tyson
@neiltyson
Astrophysicist

Neil loves to point out how science is sometimes incorrectly shown in movies, and at least one director took his criticism seriously. Neil pointed out that, in the 1997 movie *Titanic*, the Northern Crown constellation in the sky overhead as the ship *Titanic* is sinking shows the wrong number of stars. When the movie was re-released in 2012, director James Cameron corrected the stars in the constellation.

That same year, Neil also made his mark on comic book culture. In 2012, DC Comics  published issue 14 of *Action Comics*. In a story called "Star Light, Star Bright," Superman visits the Hayden Planetarium. According to the comic book, Superman visits Neil every 382 days hoping to get a glimpse of the planet Krypton, where he was born. Superman's parents sent him away from the planet right before it exploded, but because Krypton is so far away, the image of the explosion has not yet reached Earth. In the story, Superman looks through Neil's telescope at just the moment when Krypton explodes. It's a bittersweet moment for Superman.

When DC asked Neil if he would be interested in being in the story, he went one step further. He offered to find a star in the universe that

would fit. That is, a star that was the right distance away so that Superman would be seeing its destruction at the right time on Earth. Neil gave DC several stars to pick from. They chose a red star that was part of the constellation called Corvus, which means "the crow." They chose that star because the mascot of Smallville High—Superman's own high school—was a crow.

CHAPTER 10
Into the Cosmos

Back when Neil was in graduate school, he loved watching his old mentor Carl Sagan on the PBS show *Cosmos*. He loved how Sagan and the show got ordinary people excited about science. He hoped one day to do the same thing. In 2014, Fox Broadcasting decided to do a new version of *Cosmos* and they wanted Neil to host it. Of course, he was thrilled. Neil liked to say, "Science is not a subject you took in school. It's life. We are wrapped by it, in it, with it."

Neil's children, Miranda and Travis, were growing up viewing science as part of daily life. Miranda graduated from the same high school that Neil went to in New York, the Bronx High School of Science. From there, she went to college at Harvard, just like her father.

Neil's version of *Cosmos* premiered in March 2014. Like the original, it had thirteen episodes. It covered subjects from evolution to the composition of stars and global warming. Neil ended the first episode with a tribute to his old friend, Carl Sagan. He talked about Carl's work as a scientist and called him a great science communicator. Then he held up a calendar of

Carl's from 1975 and showed the page where he had scheduled a meeting with Neil, then just seventeen years old. Describing that day, Neil said, "I already knew I wanted to become a scientist, but that afternoon I learned from Carl what kind of person I wanted to become."

Neil's *Cosmos* was a hit. He was invited to speak on many talk shows, especially ones with funny hosts like Stephen Colbert and Jimmy Fallon. His show *StarTalk* expanded into television as well on the National Geographic Network.

Neil on *The Late Show with Stephen Colbert*

StarTalk created other podcasts that brought science to people in different ways. For instance, a show called *Playing with Science* used science to explain sports. Neil did an episode where he talked about the physics of wrestling. Another episode focused on the study of genetics—inherited traits—in horse racing. *StarTalk* also produced live shows in front of an audience. Neil traveled all over the country with the show, giving talks at theaters and science festivals.

In 2017, Neil, Alice, Miranda, and Travis appeared on the game show *Celebrity Family Feud* along with Neil's cousin Monique. The deGrasse Tyson family won the game, with Neil and sixteen-year-old Travis winning big in the

lightning round of fast questions. The money they won was donated to STRIVE, a charity that helps people from disadvantaged communities get the skills and education they need for good jobs.

That same year, Neil wrote *Astrophysics for People in a Hurry*. The book explained basic concepts of astrophysics in short chapters. Neil wanted to give people a way of learning about science in their spare time. While waiting for a bus or for their coffee to brew, they could learn about the universe. Neil dedicated the book to "all those who are too busy to read fat books yet nonetheless seek a conduit [a pathway] to the cosmos."

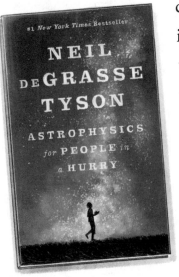

In 2018, a shadow fell over Neil's life. Three women accused him of sexual misconduct. More disturbing was the accusation of another woman who said Neil sexually assaulted her in 1984 when they were both students at the University of Texas. Neil said he was innocent of all of these crimes. The Hayden Planetarium conducted its own investigation and decided to keep Neil in his job, but there has been no police investigation.

As always, Neil decided to respond to the situation by focusing on his work.

He never stopped thinking about science as something for everyone to share and understand. He doesn't think you need to be able to do complicated math problems or have advanced degrees to appreciate how awesome and wonderful the universe is. Neil doesn't just want people to love science because he does. He believes that a deeper understanding of the world will give people the power to make it a better place.

Neil likes to say that he has been guided by two ideas: "know more today about the world than I knew yesterday and lessen the suffering of others." Through his museum work, writing, and public appearances, Neil deGrasse Tyson continues to do just that.

Timeline of Neil deGrasse Tyson's Life

1958	Born on October 5 in New York City
1967	Visits the Hayden Planetarium for the first time
1970	Gets his first telescope
1973	Sails on the SS *Canberra* to Africa
1975	Meets Carl Sagan
1980	Graduates from Harvard University
1988	Marries Alice Young
1989	Publishes *Merlin's Tour of the Universe*
1991	Earns a PhD from Columbia University
1994	Starts working for the Hayden Planetarium
1996	Becomes the director of the Hayden Planetarium
	Daughter, Miranda deGrasse Tyson, is born
1997	Begins supervising major renovation of the Hayden Planetarium
2001	Son, Travis deGrasse Tyson, is born
2014	Hosts *Cosmos: A SpaceTime Odyssey*
2017	Appears with family on episode of the game show *Celebrity Family Feud*
2019	Publishes *Letters from an Astrophysicist*

Timeline of the World

1958 — NASA founded by President Eisenhower to develop space technology for the United States

1961 — Russian cosmonaut Yuri Gagarin becomes the first man in space

1982 — Bertha Wilson appointed as first woman to sit on the Supreme Court of Canada

1992 — Divers in the Mediterranean Sea discover the sunken ancient port of Alexandria, Egypt, home of Cleopatra and Mark Antony

1994 — National Museum of the American Indian opens in New York City

2009 — Barack Obama is sworn into office as the first African American president of the United States

2014 — Malala Yousafzai becomes the youngest recipient of the Nobel Peace Prize at age seventeen for her work championing educational rights for girls in Pakistan

2019 — Sixteen-year-old Swedish climate activist Greta Thunberg speaks at the United Nations on Climate Change

2020 — Diego, a hundred-year-old Hood Island Tortoise, is released back into the wild in Española after fathering more than 900 tortoises and saving his endangered species

Bibliography

*Books for young readers

American Museum of Natural History. "Neil deGrasse Tyson on
　　Finding Krypton" (November 2012); amnh.org/explore/videos/
　　kid-science/neil-degrasse-tyson-on-finding- krypton.

*DiPrimio, Pete. *Neil deGrasse Tyson*. Kennett Square, PA: Purple
　　Toad Publishing, 2015.

MacFarlane, Seth, Ann Druyan, Brannon Braga, Mitchell Cannold,
　　Executive Producers. *Cosmos: A Spacetime Odyssey*,
　　"Episode One: Standing Up in the Milky Way." Aired March 9,
　　2014, on Fox.

Oreweg, Jessica. "Neil deGrasse Tyson Says the Moment He Fell
　　in Love with Astrophysics Came from an Embarrassing
　　Misunderstanding." *Business Insider* (May 29, 2015);
　　www.businessinsider.com/how-did-neil-degrasse-tyson
　　-become-an-astrophysicist-2015-5.

Pedas, Ted. "African Eclipse Cruise: Aboard P&O's *Canberra*, June 22–July 8, 1973." pedasfamily.com/jun22canb.html.

Prengel, Kate. "Alice Young, Neil deGrasse Tyson: Five Fast Things You Need to Know." *Heavy* (December 2, 2018); heavy.com /news/2018/12/alice-young-neil-degrasse-tysons-wife/.

*Saucier, C.A.P. *Explore the Cosmos like Neil deGrasse Tyson*. Amherst, NY: Prometheus Books, 2015.

Tyson, Neil deGrasse. *Astrophysics for People in a Hurry*. New York: W.W. Norton & Co., 2017.

Tyson, Neil deGrasse. *The Sky Is Not the Limit: Adventures of an Urban Astrophysicist*. Amherst, NY: Prometheus Books, 2004.

*Ventura, Marne. *Astrophysicist and Space Advocate: Neil deGrasse Tyson*. Minneapolis: Lerner Publications, 2014.

YOUR HEADQUARTERS FOR HISTORY

Activities, Mad Libs, and sidesplitting jokes!
Discover the Who HQ books beyond the biographies

Who? What? Where?

Learn more at whohq.com!